NEYMAR
THE NEW PELÉ

Abbeville Press Publishers

New York · London

A portion of the book's proceeds are donated to the **Hugo Bustamante AYSO Playership Fund,** a national scholarship program to help ensure that no child misses the chance to play AYSO Soccer. Donations to the fund cover the cost of registration and a uniform for a child in need.

Text by Illugi Jökulsson

For the original edition
Design: Ólafur Gunnar Guðlaugsson
Layout: Ólafur Gunnar Guðlaugsson and Árni Torfason

For the English-language edition
Editor: Nicole Lanctot
Production manager: Louise Kurtz
Layout: Ada Rodriguez
Copy editor: Jacob Field

PHOTOGRAPHY CREDITS

Getty Images: p. 2–3 (Gallo Images), 12–13 (Neymar: Jamie McDonald), 12 (Pelé: Allsport Hulton), 12 (Garrincha: Central Press), 13 (Ronaldo: Al Bello), 13 (Ronaldinho: Ben Radford), 13 (Zico: Allsport UK), 16 (Scott Heavey), 17 (Tevez: Chris McGrath), 17 (Corluka: Laurence Griffiths), 17 (Bronckhorst: Clive Mason), 17 (Hagi: Stephen Dunn), 20 (Pelé: Central Press), 22 (Lintao Zhang), 24 (Lintao Zhang), 26–27 (Julian Finney), 26 (Vinstri: Mike Hewitt), 27 (Hagri: David Ramos), 29 (Vavá/Pelé: Hulton Archive), 29 (Garrincha: Central Press), 30 (Central Press), 31 (Zico: Tony Duffy), 31 (Careca: David Cannon), 32 (Romário: Simon Bruty), 32 (Ronaldo: David Cannon), 33 (Alex Livesey), 35 (Dunga: Richard Heathcote), 35 (Menezes: Buda Mendes), 35 (Scolari: Scott Heathcote), 38–39 (Clive Rose), 38 (Dean Mouhtaropoulos), 40 (Laurence Griffiths), 41 (Laurance Griffiths), 44 (Lintao Zhang), 45 (Top: Rich Schultz), 45 (Bottom: Cris Bouroncle/AFP), 46–47 (David Ramos), 48 (Top: Adam Nurkiewicz), 48 (Right: Chris McGrath), 48 (Bottom: Adam Nurkiewicz), 49 (Left: Denis Doyle), 49 (Right: David Ramos), 50 (Maradona: David Cannon), 51 (Bale: Denis Doyle), 51 (Pelé: Allsport UK), 51 (Robben: Shaun Botterill), 51 (Zlatan: Harry Engels), 56 (David Ramos), 57 (David Ramos), 58 (Scott Heavey)

Shutterstock: p. 4 (Jefferson Bernardes), 8 (Middle: thobo), 8 (Right: Alberto Loyo), 10–11 (mangostock), 10 (Left: Catarina Belove), 10 (Right: Celso Pupo), 11 (Left: gary yim), 11 (Samo Trebizan),14 (marchello74), 17 (Ronaldo: Maxisport), 17 (Januzaj: mooinblack), 18 (Luis Carlos Torres), 21 (Robinho: Maxisport), 26 (Hagri: Celso Pupo), 34 (Celso Pupo), 36 (Rnoid), 37 (Lebron: Domenic Gareri), 37 (Smith: Andrey Bayda), 37 (Bolt: Kaliva), 42–43 (Celso Pupo), 47 (Xavi: Ververidis Vasilis), 47 (Iniesta: mooinblack), 47 (Martin: mooinblack), 50 (Messi: mooinblack), 50 (Ronaldo: Natursport), 50 (Neymar: amonfoto), 53 (mooinblack)

Wikimedia Commons: p. 8 (Left: Guilherme Gaensly), 20 (Nikolas Maciel Fabricio), 27 (Left: checkbrazil), 28 (Bottom: http://saopaulofc.in), 28 (Top: alexander2009)

Youtube: p. 23

First published in the United States of America in 2015 by Abbeville Press, 137 Varick Street, New York, NY 10013

First published in Iceland in 2014 by Sögur útgáfa, Fákafen 9, 108 Reykjavík, Iceland

First edition
10 9 8 7 6 5 4 3 2 1

ISBN 978-0-7892-1227-6

Library of Congress Cataloging-in-Publication Data available upon request

For bulk and premium sales and for text adoption procedures, write to Customer Service Manager, Abbeville Press, 137 Varick Street, New York, NY 10013, or call 1-800-ARTBOOK.

Visit Abbeville Press online at www.abbeville.com.

CONTENTS

BRAZIL

Neymar was born and raised in Brazil, which is the largest country in South America and one of the largest countries in the world. Brazil is so vast that it is possible to fit most of Europe, besides Russia, inside its borders.

Brazil has diverse landscapes. Most people are familiar with the country because of the Amazon rainforest. The extensive Amazon River has its source in the Andes and runs through the northern part of Brazil to the ocean. Several large rivers also flow into the Amazon River. At the river's widest point, it is not possible to see from one bank of the river to the other. Great forests grow in the Amazon region that are necessary for life on the planet. Many fascinating species of animals and plants thrive in the forests. The dangerous piranha lives in the Amazon!

GUYANA

FRENCH GUYANA

AMAZON BASIN
Manaus

Fortaleza

Recife

THE ANDES

BRAZIL

Salvador

Brasília

Belo Horizonte

Rio de Janeiro
São Paulo
Curitiba

Porto Alegre

SOUTH ATLANTIC

Buenos Aires   Montevideo

Italian immigrants in Brazil around the year 1900.

One of the rivers of the Amazon.

Piranha fish are only 5.5–10.25 inches long, but their teeth are sharp!

Largest countries in the world:

	Country	Size
1	Russia	6.6 million square miles
2	Canada	3.8 million square miles
3	China	3.7 million square miles
4	USA	3.7 million square miles
5	Brazil	3.3 million square miles

Largest cities in Brazil:

	City	Population
1	São Paulo	11.2 million
2	Rio de Janeiro	6.3 million
3	Salvador	2.6 million
4	Brasília	2.5 million
5	Fortaleza	2.4 million

Brasília is the capital of Brazil.

LONG HISTORY

The first humans settled in Brazil around 10,000 years ago. They originally came from Asia. Once in Brazil, they scattered all over the enormous country. Some lived by the coast while others settled in the jungles of the Amazon region. Today there are still tribes living in the Amazon in almost complete isolation who know little or nothing about the outside world.

Explorers from Europe began arriving around the year 1500 from Portugal. The people already living there had not formed any states or a single nation so the Portuguese managed to seize control of the entire area. The times were difficult for the native inhabitants. Many of them died from diseases brought to the land by the Europeans. Their culture was suppressed as thousands of immigrants came from Portugal and other European countries. Four million African slaves were transported to Brazil to work without pay on the land the Portuguese had seized. They were not freed until 1888. In 1822 Brazil gained independence from Portugal. Little by little, a new nation of Brazil began to take shape. Its roots stretched back to the original inhabitants, but the country also included European immigrants and the descendents of the African slaves.

A majority of modern-day Brazilians can trace their roots to all of those groups. For example, Neymar!

Roughly 7 billion people live on the Earth.

	Country	Population
1	China	1.354 billion
2	India	1.210 billion
3	USA	316 million
4	Indonesia	237 million
5	Brazil	193 million

The most populated country in Europe is Russia with a population of 143 million. In the larger soccer nations of Western Europe (Germany, France, England, Italy, Spain), the population is "only" between 50–80 million.

Rhode Island is the smallest state in the U.S. It is possible to fit 2,136 "Rhode Islands" into the area that Brazil covers.

A variety of struggles always arise in large and populous countries like Brazil. A significant portion of the population has always suffered from poverty and still does. Sometimes the government has not been able to help them. Now the tides are changing. Poverty has decreased and the government has improved, although things are still not perfect. The country has many natural resources as well as the riches that reside in the people themselves. Many believe that soon Brazil will become one of the world's superpowers. Despite many difficulties, present and past, Brazilians have always emphasized the joy of life. They love having fun and entertaining others and they won't allow worries to bring them down. This is why Brazilians are known for joy, passion, and lightheartedness in relation to most things—not unlike the style of the soccer they play!

COLORFUL LIFE

The famous Copacabana beach in Rio de Janeiro. People gather there to soak in the sun and socialize—and to play beach soccer!

Brazilians love festivals, especially Carnival, held every year for Mardi Gras. During Carnival, Brazilians organize mass

Though São Paulo and Rio de Janeiro are the biggest cities neither of them are the capital. Around the year 1960, Brazilians decided to build a new capital in the center of the country. The city is called Brasília. Beautiful buildings from that time period characterize the architecture of the young city.

The type of music that Brazilians are most famous for is called samba. It is soft and seems effortless, but it surges with emotion and joy under the surface. It is no surprise that Brazil's style of play is sometimes called "samba-soccer," since that is the way they want to play the game.

Most Brazilians are Catholic, though many other religions are also practiced. The famous statue of Christ above Rio de Janeiro is one of the symbols of the city and, in fact, of the whole nation.

THE MOST BEAUTIFUL SOCCER!

Brazilians love soccer. They are the most successful nation in the history of the World Cup and they demand victory every time they play in the tournament. But they also want to play with elegance and joy. It is sometimes claimed that Brazilians adhere to "jogo bonito" or "the beautiful game." They generally celebrate soccer players who are clever and dexterous and who simply enjoy the game.

The Brazilians are happiest when their idols exhibit not only fighting spirit and vitality, but also a love for the game and artistic skill. This is why the Brazilians love Neymar so much. He is extremely skillful but he also plays with passion and grace. That's how they want their stars to perform!

MORE WORLD CUP VICTORIES THAN ANY OTHER COUNTRY: BRAZILIANS BECAME WORLD CHAMPIONS IN 1958, 1962, 1970, 1994, AND 2002.

PELÉ

Became a superstar at the 1958 World Cup in Sweden and is one of the greatest soccer players in history. Pelé is the embodiment of the number 10 jersey, or the playmaker, an attacking midfielder who plays behind the forwards, controls the offense but also seeks to score as well. Still today the Brazilians seek a "new Pelé." Pelé himself has claimed that Neymar is a worthy heir.

Garrincha toys with a player from Wales in the 1958 World Cup in Sweden. Brazilians loved Garrincha for his incredible skills.

Pelé shoots for the goal in a game against Czechoslovakia during the 1970 World Cup.

GARRINCHA

Played his best game in 1962 when Brazilians became world champions for the second time. Garrincha was an almost supernaturally skilled winger, who could get the ball past anyone. Yet, one of his legs was two inches shorter than the other from birth. Neymar's father was a particular fan of Garrincha. When Neymar was a boy, his father pointed out what a great legend he was.

ZICO

He was the key player in a great Brazilian team of the '80s. Zico was a sophisticated and intelligent soccer player who could take a fantastic free kick.

RONALDO

He was probably the biggest natural talent in the history of forwards. Strong, quick, dexterous, skillful, and particularly drawn to the goal, Ronaldo had everything that a great forward needs to have.

RONALDINHO

Perhaps the most cunning and skillful player of his generation. Ronaldinho had many tricks up his sleeve and was able to exhibit such skill that his opponents were left stunned by his talent. Even though Brazilians have been able to boast of many free-kick geniuses, Ronaldinho was one of the best.

Until 2014 no one had scored as much as Ronaldo had in the finals of the World Cup.

Neymar's traits show signs of all these five legends!

Zico and companions on the Brazilian national team in 1982 and 1986 were admired for their fantastic play.

Ronaldinho was an absolute pleasure to watch on the soccer field.

13

NEYMAR'S FAMILY

Neymar's family was a completely normal middle-class family living in the suburbs of São Paulo where they lived a quiet and simple life. Neymar's father is called Neymar de Silva. He played soccer with a few lower league teams but had to retire at the age of 32 due to sustained injuries.

Neymar's father met his wife, Nadine Santos, when she was 16 years old and he was 18. They married in 1991 and a year later little Neymar came into the world.

"Little Neymar came uninvited to the wedding party; he was a two-month-old in his mother's belly, but we didn't know at the time," the father says. In 1996, his younger sister, Rafaella, was born.

The family lived with the mother of the older Neymar in a rather poor neighborhood of São Vicente, close to the big city of São Paulo. Neymar senior worked as a mechanic with the energy company CET and rode around on a motorcycle.

Today, the family lives in the beachside villa in city of Santos, which is also close to São Paulo. They own several cars and an entire yacht, which they take to sea when the weather is right. The family has therefore been through many changes, all thanks to little Neymar's soccer talents.

"My father has always been a rock. He handles everything: the money and the family," Neymar says. It was the father who first introduced Neymar to soccer and encouraged him. He introduced him to various youth teams until his son was offered a contract with the big team Santos. Today, Neymar Sr. deals with the finance and business side of his son's affairs. When soccer players become as famous and triumphant as Neymar, many companies and businesses want to be associated with them. This produces vast profits.

WHAT IS HIS FULL NAME?

Neymar da Silva Santos Júnior. The name "Neymar" is composed of the name "Ney" and "mar," which means "son of Mary." And given that his father is also called Neymar, our man is called "Júnior," which simply means "younger." In Brazil, it is common that children inherit surnames from both parents. "Da Silva" comes from Neymar's father, and from his mother Neymar got "Santos."

The name "Silva" means "forest" while "Santos" means "saints." As a result, Neymar's name could be interpreted to mean something along the lines of "Ney, Son of Mary Junior from the Forest of Saints."

Both Silva and Santos are among the most common names in Brazil and many soccer players carry these names. It is therefore not strange that Neymar refers to himself by his first name. Brazilian soccer players use their first name more often than their surname on their jerseys and in the media. Some even use nicknames, such as Pelé and Zico.

NEYMAR'S ASTROLOGICAL SIGN IS AQUARIUS.

FEBRUARY 5TH!

Neymar is not the only world-famous soccer player who has a birthday on February 5.

Cristiano Ronaldo from Portugal was born on February 5, 1985. Ronaldo became a star with Manchester United. When he played with Real Madrid it became clear that he was one of the best soccer players in the world. Thankfully Neymar did not join Real. Neymar and Ronaldo would probably argue over who should get a bigger birthday cake!

Carlos Tevez from Argentina was born on February 5, 1984. On a good day, Tevez counts among the strongest forwards in the world. After he played for both the big teams in Manchester, he was transferred to Juventus in Italy.

Vedran Corluka was born on February 5, 1986. He is a clever defender from Croatia who played for Manchester City and then Tottenham before transferring to Lokomotiv Moscow in Russia.

Giovanni van Bronckhorst was born on February 5, 1975, in the Netherlands. He was a left back and defensive midfielder who played for Arsenal and Barcelona. He is probably most famous for a magnificent goal he scored for the Dutch national team against Uruguay during the 2010 World Cup.

Gheorghe Hagi from Romania was born on February 5, 1965. Hagi was a greatly talented and daring attacking midfielder, famous for his precise passing and shooting. In the years 1990–96, Hagi played for both Real Madrid and Barcelona. And for a few years he turned the Romanian national team into a superpower.

Adnan Januzaj is a new player, an eager attacking midfielder who plays for Manchester United. He became a teenage sensation during the 2013–14 season. He is very young, born on February 5, 1995.

If these six players and Neymar formed a seven-man team, they could be coached by the Swede Sven-Göran Eriksson. He was born on February 5, 1948. Eriksson rose to fame working as a coach in Italy in the '80s and '90s and then coached the English national team with great success.

THIS IS WHERE HE COMES FROM!

São Paulo is one of the largest and most populous cities in the world. If all the suburbs and neighboring towns are counted, the total population would amount to 20 million. The city is a part of the state of São Paulo, which is the largest in Brazil, with a population of 44 million. That is more residents than in the whole of Argentina, a neighbor of Brazil!

And four times the amount of people that live in the state of Ohio!

The city of São Paulo is divided into numerous districts and neighborhoods. Around 50 miles from the city is the coast of the Atlantic Ocean. The city of Santos is situated by the coast, which is where the soccer team bearing the same name comes from. Neymar's family now lives in Santos in their villa by the ocean.

They have lived around that area since Neymar was a boy.

As with everywhere in Brazil, there is a great difference between rich and poor in São Paulo, as well as in Santos and neighboring regions. Some reside in villas and live in luxury. Others are forced to live in slums that sometimes grow up right next to the neighborhoods of the rich.

Neymar was not raised in severe poverty but early on he realized that life is not always fair. His parents could not afford their own home so they lived for a long time with Neymar's grandmother. Millions of Brazilians never manage to rise out of poverty and live in slums their entire life. These slums are called "favelas" in Brazil.

The beach in São Vicente

DISCOVERED ON THE BEACH!

The Brazilian Betinho works as a scout for Santos and travels far and wide in search of aspiring young soccer players. Betinho discovered Robinho, described on the next page, and later he discovered Neymar. "God gave me this power to discover new talents," Betinho claimed in an interview with the Spanish sports magazine sport.es. "In 1998, Neymar's father was playing in a soccer match on the beach. And I saw Neymar running around in the stands."

Betinho had forbidden his own son from running in the stands because Betinho did not want him to trip and hurt himself. "But Neymar didn't just run, he leapt. He got my attention because he was running as if on level ground, but in fact he was on the steps. I could see that the boy had talent, that he was agile and had fantastic physical coordination. It seemed genetic to me. His mother was tall and slender and the father, who was a soccer player, had a strong and robust body."

The scout immediately suspected that the boy playing on the steps would become a good soccer player.

"He stood out. The chances of a player like Neymar are one in many million. I compared him to Robinho when he was at the same age but I thought Neymar was even better. And I told his father that we had here a soccer player who would become Robinho's match at the very least."

This took place when Neymar was six years old. Betinho definitely had foresight!

And Betinho says that Neymar was not solely endowed with physical skills. "He was a cheerful boy. He has always been intelligent and did well in school. He is a player that runs, but he also thinks and observes." Neymar began training with the small team Portuguesa Santista when he was seven years old. His talents soon became clear to everyone. At the age of 11 Neymar joined the big team Santos.

Neymar's new team is one of the most famous and triumphant teams in the world. Santos's success was particularly impressive in the years 1959–75. The team won 24 titles during that time. Santos played magnificent soccer. The unparalleled Pelé was the king of the team but many other legends participated in the team's triumphs. Over this period, Santos became Brazilian champions six times. Brazilians call this legendary team Os Santásticos.

Santos's fame began to fade following the departure of Pelé and his companions from the team. Over a 20-year period, victories became a rare occurrence for the team. However, from the year 2000, the team's star started to glimmer once again. The young and fantastic Robinho carried the new team to a new era of victories.

Robinho played with joy and vitality, exactly in the way Brazilians love. Santos won two more Brazilian championships. When Robinho transferred to Real Madrid, there was another decline in the fortunes of Santos, but in 2009, the team was again soaring.

Two young boys began playing with the team and made their breakthrough there, namely, Neymar and the attacking midfielder Ganso. Despite their young age, they led Santos to various great victories.

The Brazilians were most content with the fact that the team played exemplary offensive soccer, with its samba rhythms and Neymar's speed and shot accuracy.

PELÉ

Began playing with Santos in 1956 and starred for the team until 1974. Pelé played 656 competition soccer games for Santos and scored 643 goals. Santos also hosted friendly games around the world and if these are also counted, then Pelé played a total of 1,115 games and scored 1,088 goals!

Pelé

Robinho

ROBINHO

Was born in 1984. Robinho began playing with Santos when he was 18 years old and remained with the team for three years. He played 141 games and scored 61 goals. The collaboration between Robinho and the attacking midfielder Diego is well-known. At a very young age, Robinho was already the key player in the Brazilian national team. For a time it appeared as if Robinho would join the ranks of the world's greatest soccer players, but he never reached that far. He did however play with fantastic teams such as Real Madrid, Manchester City, and AC Milan and always delivered his best. Robinho is still much loved at Santos for his contribution to the team in his younger days.

NEYMAR

Played a total of 225 games with Santos in 2009–13. Neymar scored a total of 136 goals!

Santos means "the Saints."

45 Santos players have played with Brazilian national teams at the World Cup. Of that group, 11 have become world champions!

WITH SANTOS

Carles Puyol tries to restrain Neymar in a game between Barcelona and Santos in the FIFA World Cup.

Neymar played his first competitive game for Santos's first team on March 7, 2009, when he had just turned 17 years old. The game was against Oeste Futebol Clube in a competition of teams from the state of São Paulo. Neymar entered the field from the bench and participated for the final thirty minutes. A week later, on March 16, he scored his first goal in a 3–0 victory against Mogi Mirim. Neymar dashed toward the defense, passed to the wing, received a pass back and then managed to score. Quick and precise, classic Neymar! Despite his young age, Neymar displayed great skills from the onset and played 48 games during the season and scored 14 goals.

Santos won the tournament, which is called the Campeonato Paulista.

The following year, Neymar continued to rack up goals and scored 42 goals in 60 games, at the tender age of 18. It was now clear that a genius had entered the stage. Neymar was not just accumulating goals, but each goal was more spectacular than the last. He also had an extremely high level of understanding of the game. When discussions arose regarding a potential move to a European club, he responded by saying that for the time being he intended to play only for Santos!

However, Neymar simultaneously revealed that playing in Europe was his dream.

CLOSE TO REAL MADRID

When Neymar had just turned 14 years old, he embarked on a journey which could have been fateful. He traveled to Madrid and presented himself to the legendary team Real. The managers of the youth activities at Real Madrid saw what he was capable of and wanted him to join them. This was an adventurous experience for the young Neymar. At the time, Real had world-famous geniuses in its ranks such as Zidane, Raúl, and Beckham. Also starring for them were Neymar's countrymen Roberto Carlos and the great goalscorer Ronaldo. Not to mention Robinho, who had arrived from Santos the previous year. But just before Neymar's father was about to sign the contract, Santos intervened. The team offered such a vast amount of money that Neymar's family could safely reject Real's offer. So, Neymar stayed in Brazil!

What would have happened to Neymar if his career as a soccer player had been shaped with Real Madrid?

Neymar interviewed at the age of 13.

Neymar's amazing skills at the age of 14.

Neymar is here wearing the Santos jersey, battling for the ball with Ryoichi Kurisawa, a player from Kashiwa Reysol. The game took place in December 2011, and was part of the FIFA World Cup, which was held in Japan.

CHAMPION IN SOUTH AMERICA

In 2011, Neymar's goal scoring was not as impressive as the year before, with 23 goals in 47 games. Most people would still be delighted with those figures! But still his talents became more obvious and Neymar contributed a whole lot to Santos's triumphs during that year. The team won the Campeonato Paulista for the second consecutive year. Paulista is a league championship consisting of teams from the state of São Paulo. That year Santos also won the Copa Libertadores. This is a tournament for South America's top teams, similar to the UEFA Champions League. In the six games of the group stages Neymar scored three goals and Santos qualified for the knockout stage. Santos defeated the América team from Mexico in the 16-team phase and was then eliminated by Once Caldas from Colombia in the quarterfinals. There, Neymar scored the goal that secured the victory.

In the semifinals, Santos defeated Cerro Porteño from Paraguay and once again Neymar scored. This was followed by two games for the title against Peñarol from Uruguay. The first game, which took place in Uruguay, was a goalless draw. During the beginning of the second half of the second game on Santos's home field, Neymar was the difference between the teams. He received the ball on the left side of the penalty box and made a lightning quick shot that the Peñarol goalkeeper was incapable of stopping. After this, it was clear that Santos would win their first Copa Libertadores title since the days of Pelé in 1963.

Neymar was chosen the player of the game! Neymar and Pelé fell into an embrace after the game.

TIME FOR GOOD-BYES

In 2012, Neymar scored 47 goals, as he had done in 2010. He was the star player for Santos, who won the Campeonato Paulista for the third year in a row. However, Santos was eliminated from the Copa Libertadores in the semifinals. The 2013 season also began with a bang—but now the time had come for departure!

THE HAIR!

Neymar has attracted attention for his hairstyles ever since he first entered the spotlight. Young boys around the world arrive at salons holding pictures of Neymar and want the same hairstyle. Adult soccer players have even been spotted with hairstyles that are obviously influenced by the young Brazilian.

To begin with, Neymar often cut his hair into a "Mohawk" of various shapes, but later the hairstyles became more diverse. It is safe to say that once Neymar is properly established as a superstar of the Spanish soccer world, there will be an increase of young boys entering the barbershop with images of Neymar in their pockets!

FEBRUARY 6, 2013

Neymar in a game against England at Wembley Stadium.

JUNE 26, 2013

Neymar with the Brazilian national team in a game against Uruguay during the Confederations Cup.

JULY 20, 2012

Neymar wore a headband when Brazil faced Great Britain in a friendly match before the 2012 London Olympics.

When Real Madrid was interested in signing Neymar, officials from the team flew to Brazil in order to discuss a contract with Santos and the player. One of Real's requests was that Neymar would abandon his wild hairstyles!

OCTOBER 30, 2011

SEPTEMBER 14, 2013

Neymar sporting a Mohawk at a Red Bulls match.

Neymar's hair was short when he arrived at Barcelona.

BRAZIL AT THE WORLD CUP!

BRAZIL IS THE ONLY NATIONAL TEAM THAT HAS PARTICIPATED IN EVERY WORLD CUP SINCE THE BEGINNING OF THE TOURNAMENT.

1930

The tournament was held in Uruguay. Argentina was defeated by the host country 4–2 in the finals. Brazil failed to make it out of the group stages.

1934

Italy, who hosted the tournament, defeated Czechoslovakia 2–1 in the final. Brazil was knocked out of the tournament after one game against Spain.

1938

Italy defended its title in France and beat Hungary 4–2 in the final. The Brazilian team defeated Sweden 4–2 in a match for third place. Leônidas became Brazil's first World Cup star and was the tournament's top goalscorer with seven goals in four games.

Best player of the tournament: Leônidas, Brazil.

1950

Brazil hoped for victory on its home field but unexpectedly lost the last game against Uruguay 1–2. Uruguay gained their second title as world champions. Ademir was the top goalscorer with eight goals in six games. Geniuses such as Zizinho, Jair, and Chico all performed extremely well but it was not enough to bring them victory. The defeat was a tremendous shock for Brazil.

Best player of the tournament: Zizinho, Brazil.

1954

Brazil lost to the powerful Hungarian team in the semifinals. The tournament took place in Switzerland and the match came to be known as the "Battle of Berne" due to the ferocity of the game. West Germany defeated Hungary 3–2 in the final.

1958

Now the time had come for Brazil's much deserved victory. Their performance topped every other team and the 17-year-old Pelé charmed everyone with an incredible show of skill. The Brazilians won a 5–2 victory over Sweden in the final.

1st World Cup Title
June 29, 1958
Råsunda Stadium, Solna, Sweden
BRAZIL VS. SWEDEN
5–2

Vavá 9, 32	Liedholm 4
Pelé 55, 90	Simonsson 80
Zagallo 68	

Gilmar
Djalma Santos – Orlando – Bellini – Nílton Santos
Zito – Didi
Garrincha – Vavá – Pelé – Zagallo

Coach: Vicente Feola

Pelé and Vavá

1962

Brazil confidently defended the title and defeated Czechoslovakia 3–1 in the final. The tournament was held in Chile. Pelé was injured early in the tournament but Vavá and especially Garrincha carried the torch for Brazil. Vavá and Garrincha were in the group of top goalscorers with four goals each.

Best player: Garrincha, Brazil

2nd World Cup Title
June 17, 1962
Estadio Nacional, Santiago, Chile
BRAZIL VS. CZECHOSLOVAKIA
3–1

Amarildo 17	Masopust 15
Zito 69	
Vavá 78	

Gilmar
Djalma Santos – Mauro – Zozimo – Nílton Santos
Zito – Didi
Garrincha – Vavá – Amarildo – Zagallo

Coach: Aymoré Moreira

1966

This is the tournament that Brazilians have tried to forget. The team lacked spirit and failed to rise out of the group stages. England, the hosts of the tournament, won their first and only World Cup title when they defeated West Germany 4–2.

1970

The tournament was held in Mexico. Brazil claimed the richly deserved title following a 4–1 victory over Italy in the final. Pelé was once again in top form and the entire team delivered a top performance, led by team captain Carlos Alberto and the midfield machine Gérson. Moreover, Jairzinho achieved the fantastic feat of scoring a goal in all the games he participated in, a total of seven goals in six games. Best player of the tournament: Pelé, Brazil.

Jairzinho

3rd World Cup Title
June 21, 1970
Azteca Stadium, Mexico City, Mexico

BRAZIL VS. ITALY
4–1

Pelé 18	Boninsegna 37
Gérson 66	
Jairzinho 71	
Carlos Alberto 86	

Félix
Carlos Alberto – Brito – Piazza – Everaldo
Gérson – Clodoaldo
Jairzinho – Tostao – Pelé – Rivelino

Coach: Mário Zagallo

1974

The tournament was held in West Germany and the host nation beat the fabulous Dutch team 2–1 in the final. The Brazilian team seemed slightly sluggish without Pelé but managed to make the third place playoff, where they lost 0–1 to Poland.

1978

The tournament was held in Argentina. The hosts defeated the Netherlands 3–1 in the final. Brazil's performance was noteworthy because the team lost none of their matches. They managed to gain third place with a 2–1 victory over Italy. The Brazilian team was powerful but lacked the soccer geniuses that could have made a winning difference.

1982

The tournament was held in Spain. Italy defeated West Germany in the final 3–1. Earlier in the tournament Italy had knocked out Brazil. Soccer fans were extremely disappointed with this turn of events, given that the Brazilian team was exceptionally strong and their team was one of the most entertaining in World Cup history. Legends like Zico, Sócrates, and Falcão were a pleasure to watch, however, the team was short a reliable goalscorer.

1986

Zico, Sócrates, and companions were once again knocked out of the tournament despite wowing the fans. The great forward Careca scored five goals in the tournament. Brazil lost in a penalty shootout in the quarterfinals to France after a 1–1 tie, in an entertaining game. The renowned Telê Santana coached Brazil as he had done four years before.

Zico

Argentina, led by Maradona, won the world championship title by beating West Germany 3–2.

1990

This was one of the least entertaining World Cup tournaments of all time and probably Brazil's least exciting national team. They were knocked out in the round of 16 by Argentina. West Germany defeated Argentina 1–0 in perhaps the dullest World Cup final in history.

1994

The United States hosted this tournament. Finally, Brazil managed to reclaim the title they had last held in 1970. The team's play was perhaps not at its most elegant, but they were successful and the forwards Romário and Bebeto took care of the goal scoring. However, in the final against Italy, a penalty shootout was necessary to determine the winner. Best player of the tournament: Romário, Brazil.

Careca

4th World Cup Title
July 17, 1994
Rose Bowl, Pasadena, USA

BRAZIL VS. ITALY

0–0
(3–2)*

* After thirty minutes of overtime, a penalty shootout was held to decide the winner. Romário, Branco, and Dunga scored for Brazil.

Taffarel
Jorginho (Cafu 21) – Aldair – Márcio Santos – Branco
Mazinho – Mauro Silva – Dunga – Zinho (Viola 106)
Romário – Bebeto

Coach: Carlos Alberto Parreria

Romário

Ronaldo was dangerous on the field!

1998

The strong Brazilian team was seemingly on the path to victory in this tournament held in France. The young genius Ronaldo was a sensation. In the final against France, Ronaldo was weakened after he suffered seizures in the morning before the match. The Brazilians were therefore an easy prey for the fierce French team. France won 3–0. Ronaldo was nevertheless chosen the best player of the tournament.

2002

The tournament was held in Japan and South Korea. The Brazilians won a deserved victory over Germany in the final. The Brazilian team was equipped with powerful forwards, Ronaldo was in his best form and he was the tournament's top goalscorer with eight goals. Rivaldo scored five goals and the young Ronaldinho showed great agility and skill. Behind them, the attacking fullbacks Cafu and Roberto Carlos formed a steady backbone. Cafu played in his third final in a row.

Rivaldo and Ronaldo celebrate. To the right is the hard-working midfielder Gilberto Silva.

2006

Italy defeated France in a penalty shootout to win the final. The Brazilians appeared spent after they lost to France 0–1 in the semifinals.

5th World Cup Title
June 30, 2002
The International Stadium, Yokohama, Japan

BRAZIL VS. GERMANY
2–0

Ronaldo 67, 79

Marcos
Lúcio – Edmílson – Roque Júnior
Cafu – Gilberto Silva – Kléberson – Roberto Carlos
Rivaldo – Ronaldo (Denílson 90) – Ronaldinho
(Juninho Paulista 85)

Coach: Luiz Felipe Scolari

2010

The first ever World Cup finals held in Africa. Spain won a 1–0 victory over the Netherlands in the final. Brazil was once again knocked out in the semifinals by the very team that lost in the final, the Netherlands. The final score was 1–2. Brazil hoped that their roster of forwards, Luís Fabiano, Robinho, and Kaká, would match the performance of earlier legends but the team never reached its potential. Unfortunately, Neymar was not a member of the team.

2014

Brazilians eagerly anticipated this year's World Cup, set in their home country. Held in twelve cities, including Rio de Janeiro, Brasília, and São Paulo, the tournament took a dramatic turn for Brazil's national team. In the semifinals, Germany beat Brazil 7–1, the worst loss in the country's history since 1920. (Oscar scored the lone goal.) Germany would go on to win the World Cup 1–0 in the final against Argentina.

CHOSEN FOR THE NATIONAL TEAM!

In the spring of 2011 Brazilians were preparing for the World Cup in South Africa. Many believed that the team, assembled by coach Dunga, lacked a daring offense and attacking prowess. The 18-year-old Neymar had attracted attention both with Santos and the junior national teams of Brazil. Many therefore wanted him to play for the senior national team in the World Cup. As well as Neymar, they also wanted his companion from Santos, the midfielder Ganso. Thousands of people signed a petition addressed to Dunga that called for their participation. Famous geniuses like Pelé and Romário also encouraged Dunga to choose Neymar, and a Brazilian TV station made a whole show dedicated just to this topic—and aired it from the street outside Dunga's home! Dunga however did not budge and claimed that Neymar was still too inexperienced. Then he called the police to boot the people out of the TV station!

Dunga did not show the same courage as Feola, the coach who accepted the 17-year-old Pelé for the 1958 World Cup in Sweden, where the adolescent was a hit. Maybe Neymar would have been able to invigorate a rather uncreative Brazilian team in the 2010 World Cup. The team was knocked out in the quarterfinals, since they were desperately lacking in flair and attacking skill.

After the World Cup Dunga was fired and a new coach was hired. His name was Mano Menezes. One of his first choices was to select Neymar for the team. He played his first national game on August 10, 2012, against the U.S. As if to show Dunga his mistake in not picking him, Neymar scored a goal and Brazil defeated the United States 2–0.

Unfortunately, Menezes was unable to achieve success. Neymar and his companions competed in the 2011 Copa América (a tournament for national teams in South America) but were eliminated in the semifinals. Neymar scored two goals and his performance was at times stellar, but it was not enough to keep Brazil in the tournament. In August 2012, he traveled with the Brazilian under-23 team to the London Olympics. Brazil was determined to win the only international title they had yet to obtain. But this was not to be. Mexico defeated the Brazilian team 2–1 in the final. Neymar had performed well, scored three goals in the tournament, including one from a beautiful free kick. Neymar was increasingly the first choice to take free kicks in offensive situations. Menezes was fired following the tournament and the veteran coach Luis Felipe Scolari was hired in his place. Scolari had made Brazil world champions in 2002, but failed to repeat the victory at the 2014 World Cup. (Dunga was reinstated as Brazil's manager after Scolari's unsuccessful 2014 run.) In 2002, Scolari had the legend Ronaldo in his team, who racked up many goals.

Now, he had Neymar! Even though Brazil did not win in 2014, Neymar was short-listed for FIFA's Golden Ball award as the best player of the tournament—and he was the third top goalscorer.

THREE OF NEYMAR'S COACHES IN THE NATIONAL TEAM:

DUNGA

MENEZES

SCOLARI

Neymar in a game against Uruguay in the 2013 Confederations Cup, held in Belo Horizonte.

As of October 14, 2014, Neymar has played 58 national games and scored 40 goals, which places him on the list of Brazil's top five goalscorers of all time. Here is that list:

	Name	Goals	Games
1	Pelé	77	92
2	Ronaldo	62	98
3	Romário	55	70
4	Zico	52	72
5	Neymar	40	58

THE PERSON

MOTTO

"Courage and joy. The words describe my personality well but also the soccer player, because when I play, I always try to show courage and joy."

TEMPERAMENT

Neymar says that he is always smiling, glad, and in a good mood except for rare moments when he allows little things to frustrate him. But Neymar is always quick to shake off a bad mood.

THE HAPPIEST

Neymar is happiest with his family and surrounded with friends. Neymar and his friends play video games together and watch movies and TV shows.

FAVORITES

The TV series *Two and a Half Men* is his favorite and so are the *Spider-Man* films. Neymar also loves Will Smith's movies.

ADMIRES LEBRON AND BOLT!

Neymar also watches sports on TV and not only soccer. He is a great admirer of the basketball star LeBron James and the Jamaican sprinter Usain Bolt.

LeBron James

Will Smith

Usain Bolt

MONEY

Neymar claims he is not motivated by money. The most important thing he has bought was a home for his parents. Neymar enjoys spending time in the house with his family.

FAVORITE FOOD

Neymar loves eating Brazilian home cooking including dishes with rice, beans, beef, and sweet potatoes.

THE MOST IMPORTANT GADGET

For Neymar, a smartphone is vital. If there was a fire and Neymar could only save one object, he would choose his smartphone. He says he mainly uses the phone for social media sites on the Internet, but he is a bit lazy when it comes to actually speaking on the phone!

NUMBER 10 IN THE CONFEDERATIONS CUP

Neymar celebrates a goal in a match against Japan in the Confederations Cup on June 15, 2013.

In June 2013, the FIFA Confederations Cup was held in Brazil. This tournament features the national champions from each continent. Neymar was eager to become the number 10 of the Brazilian national team. He longed to show in a major tournament that he was a worthy heir to Pelé, Zico, Ronaldinho, and other legends that had previously worn this number. Some believed Neymar was not ready. Scolari, the new coach of the national team, trusted the young man. Neymar entered the first game against Japan wearing the number 10 jersey.

The number seemed to have a positive effect on Neymar. In the third minute, Marcelo crossed the ball, which was then chested down by Fred to Neymar, who volleyed the ball right outside the penalty box, slamming it past the Japanese goalkeeper. This fantastic goal set the tone for what was come to later. Neymar was influential all over the field and Brazil won 3–0.

Brazil defeated Mexico 2–0 in the following game and Neymar scored the first goal in the ninth minute. The ball fell to Neymar from a Mexican defender. Seizing his chance, Neymar blasted the ball into the net. In the final game of the group stages, Neymar and his teammates faced difficult opponents, the powerful Italian team. Neymar scored a tremendous goal from a free kick, which gave Brazil a 2–1 lead. The game ended with Brazil winning 4–2.

Neymar was chosen the man of the match for all three games.

During the semifinals, the Brazilians defeated a ferocious Uruguay team. Neymar did not score but continued his fantastic form. The young man had obviously become a real leader on the field! But would he be able to withstand the pressure in the final?

Neymar scores a goal against Mexico.

THE BEST!

Neymar raises the trophy after leading Brazil to victory in the Confederations Cup. Brazil defeated Spain on June 30 at the Maracanã Stadium in Rio de Janeiro.

On June 30, 2013, Neymar showed the soccer world that a new genius had emerged. He led the Brazilian team in a game against Spain in the finals of the FIFA Confederations Cup. The game was held at the famous Maracanã Stadium in Rio de Janeiro, the stage of two World Cup finals (1950 and 2014). The mighty Spanish team had already won three major tournaments in a row: the UEFA European Championship in 2008 and 2012, and the 2010 World Cup. They arrived with their most powerful team. The starting lineup included six of Neymar's future teammates at Barcelona: Xavi, Iniesta, Busquets, Piqué, Jordi Alba, and Pedro. However, Spain was unable to achieve victory. Brazil defeated the world and European champions 3–0. Neymar scored a beautiful goal in the 44th minute. Oscar provided the assist with a sweet pass through the Spanish defense. The determined striker Fred scored the other two goals, with Neymar playing a part in both.

Neymar was chosen the man of the match in the final. He then received the Bronze Boot as the tournament's third top goalscorer. Neymar and his companions picked up the winning trophy. To cap it off, Neymar was awarded the Golden Ball as BEST PLAYER OF THE TOURNAMENT!

Neymar scores his goal against Spain.

EVERYBODY WANTED NEYMAR

Many Real Madrid fans dreamed of witnessing this: Neymar wearing the team jersey.

The first team that sought the services of Neymar (aside from Real Madrid when he was 14) was, strangely enough, the English team West Ham. The team had barely managed to escape relegation from the English Premier League during the spring of 2010. After the season ended, they made an $18 million offer to buy Neymar from Santos. West Ham's bid was immediately rejected as well as another offer of $30 million, which came a little later from the wealthy team Chelsea. In the summer of 2011, Real Madrid once again tried to grab Neymar.

Santos of course wanted to keep Neymar for as long as they could. The team increased his salary in order to hold onto him. However, it was clear that Neymar would be sold to a top European team sooner rather than later.

Brazilians hoped that Neymar would play in his home country at least until the 2014 World Cup in Brazil

was over. By the spring of 2013, it was clear that this would not be the case.

Neymar needed to participate with a stronger team than Santos, in order to continue his development as a player. Several teams were rumored to be interested in signing him. Chelsea's interest was rekindled and discussions arose concerning the curiosity of other rich teams, such as Manchester City and Paris Saint Germain. However, Neymar only wanted to play with a Spanish team.

As before, Real Madrid did not try to hide its interest. Neymar had often declared his admiration for the Real Madrid forward Cristiano Ronaldo. The team's managers hoped that Neymar would find the idea of playing with Ronaldo enticing. It was then a public secret that Neymar's biggest wish was to join Barcelona. Late in May 2013, news began to spread claiming that Neymar was on his way to Barcelona!

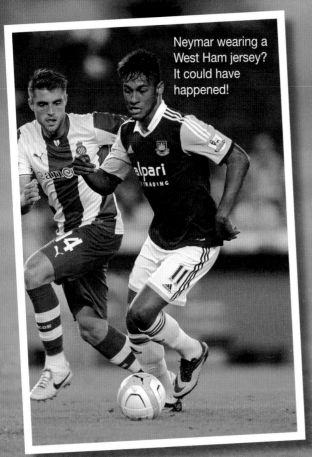

Neymar wearing a West Ham jersey? It could have happened!

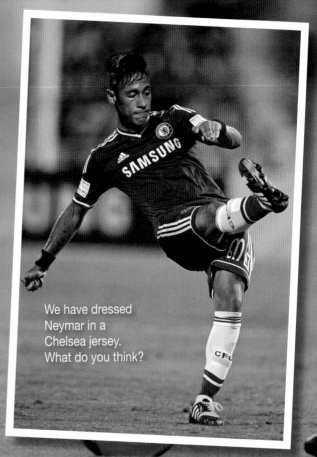

We have dressed Neymar in a Chelsea jersey. What do you think?

NEYMAR AND MESSI

It is safe to say that most people were burning with anticipation when they heard that Neymar had joined Barcelona. The idea that Neymar and the Argentinian genius Messi would work together was particularly appealing.

Not everyone was convinced that the pair could cooperate. The old Dutch legend Johan Cruyff had his doubts. He even suggested that it was time for Barcelona to sell Messi because Neymar had arrived!

Messi did not agree with this idea.

"I'm sure he will be a good signing for what we want to achieve," Messi said to journalists. "Hopefully Neymar can make a big contribution to Barcelona and can continue to demonstrate the sort of performances that he's shown for Brazil and Santos."

The relationship between Neymar and Messi was always good when they met on the field.

Next, the champions met in a friendly game between Brazil and Argentina on June 9, 2012. The game took place in New Jersey. In a highly thrilling game, Neymar made two assists but Messi scored a hat trick and secured Argentina a 4–3 victory.

In the summer of 2013, Neymar and Messi met once again in a charity game that took place in Lima in Peru on July 2, 2013. There, "Messi and friends" faced a team of superstars, which included Neymar. The game was first and foremost friendly and uncompetitive and ended with an 8–5 victory for Messi and his team. Messi and Neymar scored two goals each. Neymar scored a fantastic goal almost from midfield!

Lionel Messi was born in Argentina in 1987. Messi has played with Barcelona since the beginning of his professional career and is acknowledged as one of the world's greatest soccer players.

BARCELONA!

The team that Neymar joined is one of the giants of European soccer. Barcelona has a long history and is continuously battling the other top Spanish team, Real Madrid, for dominance. Recent years have been particularly successful. From the 2004–05 season, Barcelona has won the Spanish premier league, La Liga, six times out of ten. Since 2006, Barcelona has won the UEFA Champions League three times.

The team has made these achievements by playing beautiful soccer. The Barcelona style emphasizes graceful soccer with short passes, accurate play, and elegant goals. This kind of soccer they call "tiki-taka."

CAMP NOU

Barça's home field is much feared by players from other teams. The atmosphere in the stadium is unforgettable, which is no surprise since it has room for 99,786 people. It is Europe's largest stadium.

THE COACH

Barcelona's coach is Luis Enrique. He was born in 1970 in Spain. He started his soccer career with Sporting Gijón before playing for Real Madrid and Barcelona. He also played for the Spanish national team. He retired as a player in 2004 and became a coach. Before he got the job at Barcelona in May 2014, Luis Enrique coached AS Roma and Celta Vigo.

THE TEAMMATES

No team has as many soccer geniuses as Barcelona! At the top is Lionel Messi (b. 1987). Xavi (b. 1980) controls the midfield. He and Iniesta (b. 1984) are embodiments of the great tiki-taka style of soccer. With Neymar on board, the artistry of these players has been elevated to even greater heights!

BARCELONA'S TITLES

La Liga	22 times
Copa del Rey	26 times
UEFA Champions League	4 times
FIFA World Cup	2 times

Xavi

Iniesta

Luis Enrique

FRANCE

SPAIN

CATALONIA

Madrid

Barcelona

Valencia

Seville

MEDITERRANEAN SEA

Neymar celebrates after scoring the first goal in a match between Barcelona and Real Madrid in Camp Nou on October 26, 2013. Dani Alves, an adventurous right back and Neymar's teammate for Barcelona and the Brazilian national team, is also euphoric!

47

Łukasz Kacprzycki from Lechia Gdańsk tries to stop Neymar in a friendly game on July 30, 2013. This was Neymar's first game wearing the Barcelona jersey.

The first goal! Neymar celebrates with Fabregas after scoring a goal against the Thai team on August 7, 2013.

A historic moment. Neymar waiting to enter his first game with Barcelona just before he was substituted for Alexis Sánchez.

FIRST GAMES WITH BARÇA

July 30, 2013, was an average Tuesday for most people. However, in the eyes of soccer fans it was particularly significant. On that day, Neymar played for the first time in a Barcelona jersey. He was substituted for Alexis Sánchez in the 78th minute in a friendly game where Barça met with Polish team Lechia Gdańsk. The Poles were playing at home. The score was 2–2 following goals by Sergi Roberto and Lionel Messi against the Polish team, which had twice gained the lead.

Lionel Messi was substituted just before Neymar, so they did not play together in the game. The young Brazilian played for 15 minutes, mainly on the left wing. He performed well but failed to secure a goal and the 2–2 score remained unchanged. After the game, Neymar was congratulated by everyone for achieving this milestone!

Neymar scored his first goal for Barcelona on August 7 in a 7–1 victory against the Thai national team in a friendly game.

In Neymar's first official game for Barça he entered the field in the 63th minute in a game against Levante. Barcelona won the game 7–0. Neymar did not manage to score. Neymar did not score his first real goal until August 21 when Barcelona faced Atlético Madrid in the Super Cup of Spain. Neymar's goal was decisive in contributing to Barcelona's victory in this tournament!

The young man was making a name for himself in Barcelona!

The first goal in a competitive game. Neymar shoots the ball past Thibaut Courtois, the goalkeeper of Atlético Madrid, in a match for the Spanish Super Cup.

Neymar as he waits to come onto the field for his first appearance in La Liga. The match took place on August 18, 2013.

HOW TALL IS HE?

HEIGHT UNDER THE BAR: 8 FEET

LIONEL
MESSI
5' 7"

CRISTIANO
RONALDO
6' 1"

NEYMAR
5' 9"

DIEGO
MARADONA
5' 5"

Size does not matter when it comes to soccer as it is easy to see. Neymar is among the tallest in the Barcelona squad, since many of the other important players on the team are less than six feet tall. Pedro is 5 feet 6½ inches; and Messi, Xavi, Jordi Alba, and Iniesta are all 5 feet 7 inches. Luis Suárez is 5 feet 11 inches, Mascherano is 5 feet 7½ inches, and Dani Alves is 5 feet 9 inches—just like Neymar. The tallest Barcelona players are Piqué (6 feet 4 inches) and Jérémy Mathieu (6 feet 3 inches).

GARETH
BALE
6'

PELÉ
5' 8"

ARJEN
ROBBEN
5' 11"

ZLATAN
IBRAHIMOVIĆ
6' 5"

WHAT IS HE GOOD AT?

AND IS HE BAD AT SOMETHING?!

SPEED

He is one of the quickest. Maybe not as lightning-quick as Gareth Bale, but close. Neymar exercises great control of speed, and the ball seems glued to his shoe even though he is running at full speed.

DRIBBLING

There are few who exceed Neymar when it comes to dribbling, even at great speed. In these circumstances, Neymar has incredible control over the ball. When it comes to getting past defenders, Neymar is simply one of the greatest in the world.

HEADER TECHNIQUE

Still not Neymar's strong side. Given his short stature, he is not famed for his heading techniques. Neymar will doubtlessly work on improving this. It is worth mentioning that Messi, who is even shorter than Neymar, has managed to score a number of important headers.

LONG SHOTS

Simply great. Neymar has scored fantastic goals via long shots. He is always prepared to take a shot as he moves closer to the opponent's penalty box.

FREE KICK

At the start, Neymar was not a free kick master. He has put tremendous effort into improving his free kick, and with great results. His progress in this area shows that he does not quit until he has reached his goal.

UNDERSTANDING OF GAME

Extremely deep. Neymar has great vision and seems to always know where the ball is headed. Given that an advanced understanding of the game does not develop until a player's early twenties, it seems like Neymar has the opportunity to progress even further!

FINISHING

Neymar is fantastic when it comes to this. He can score from almost any location, inside and outside the penalty box. He has scored from extremely tight angles.

COOPERATION

In the beginning, Neymar was often accused of selfishness. This is a problem that all young geniuses have to face. Why should I pass to someone else if I know that no one can do it better than me? This is something people have to learn and there are no places better than the Brazilian national team and Barcelona when it comes to lessons on cooperation.

CHARACTER

If strong defenders would cover Neymar tightly in the past he would sometimes almost disappear from the game. He seemed to struggle with aggressive opponents. His performance at the 2013 Confederations Cup proved that this was no longer the case.

MOOD

In the worst of times Neymar could become frustrated. When he met with adversity, he could grow angry and irritated, but he is working on this. Most of the time, the joy and pleasure Neymar gets from playing soccer are clear to see.

10 FACTS

On April 6, 2011, Neymar played for Santos against Colo Colo from Chile in the Copa Libertadores, the South American championship. Neymar scored a fabulous goal by slipping past four defenders before dinking the ball over the goalkeeper. The audience went wild with cheers and one of them threw a Neymar mask onto the field. The masks had been distributed among the fans before the match. In a state of exaltation Neymar put on the mask (in fact upside down) and was given a yellow card by the referee. Neymar persistently objected but apparently it is stated in the rules that masks are forbidden during game play. Neymar had no clue about this. What was worse was that he had been given a yellow card earlier in the game and was therefore sent off. This caused such an uproar that by the end of the game the referee had sent off three more players!

Few athletes, let alone Brazilian ones, make it onto the cover of *Time*, not even Pelé. Neymar achieved this in March 2013. Like so many times before, he was dubbed "the next Pelé" on the cover.

Neymar's first game with Santos was against Oeste on March 7, 2009, in the Campeonato Paulista. He had just turned 17. Neymar scored his first goal eight days later, on March 15, when Santos defeated Mogi Mirim 3–0 in the same tournament.

When Chelsea made an offer for Neymar in 2010, Pelé himself called Neymar's father and nearly begged him to convince Neymar to stay with Santos for the time being. After a 15-minute conversation, Pelé got his way. What would you do if Pelé called you?

At the beginning of his career, Neymar was often accused of intentionally tripping, or

China's Hackers / The World's Hardest Job / Lethal TB

TIME

How the career of Brazilian football star **Neymar** explains his country's economy

The Next Pelé

BY BOBBY GHOSH

diving, when an opponent came near. This had a grain of truth. Pelé is said to have encouraged Neymar to lay off all theatrics. Neymar is still often subjected to unfair treatment by defenders of the opposing team.

The day that Neymar turned 20, on February 5, 2012, he scored a goal against Palmeiras in the Campeonato Paulista. This was his 100th goal with Santos and the Brazilian national team.

On August 15, 2012, Neymar played in a friendly game with the Brazilian Olympic team against Sweden in Stockholm. Neymar did not score a goal but Brazil won 3–0. Immediately after the game was over, he hopped into a private jet and played an important game the following day for Santos against Figueirense in the Brazilian Championship. Neymar was criticized for the erratic behavior, but nevertheless performed well in both games.

Neymar scored three great goals and made an assist for the fourth when Santos won a victory over Cruzeiro in a game during the Brazilian Championship on November 3, 2012. Neymar's performance was so brilliant that Cruzeiro fans gave him special applause at the end of the game. He was deeply touched and said: "From now on Cruzeiro will become my second home."

Neymar really enjoys listening to music and dancing. He is particularly fond of "Música sertaneja," which is traditional Brazilian pop music. In 2011, the singer Michel Teló made it big in South America with the song "Ai se eu te pego." In the famous music video for the song, Neymar shows his skills, both on the soccer field and dancing in the changing room. Neymar has also appeared in other music videos for Brazilian musicians.

In April 2013, a Brazilian comic was published that revolved around the boy Neymar and his adventures. The stories are illustrated by one of Brazil's most famous comic book authors. Neymar was very happy with this development!

The comic-book Neymar exhibits his skills.

FAMILY MAN

Neymar and Messi held their sons as they pose for photographers before a match against Real Sociedad in La Liga on September 24, 2013. Davi Lucca had just turned two, and Thíago, Messi's son, was nine months old.

BECOMES A FATHER!

Neymar became a father on August 24, 2011, when his son was born. Neymar was only 19 years old at the time. The mother was 18 years old. She did not care for the attention of the media spotlight and Neymar asked everyone to respect this. They did not want to be a couple, but he bought a fabulous house for the mother of his son, where she now lives.

Neymar declared publicly that at first he had felt a strong sense of responsibility in becoming a father—and he was not certain as to how he would handle this responsibility. Neymar quickly arrived at the conclusion that his son was a gift from God, which he sincerely celebrated. When his son came into the world Neymar was ecstatic. He said that the boy was "five pounds of pure happiness." The boy was christened Davi Lucca. Neymar cares for the boy very much. Davi celebrated his second birthday around the same time that his father began his first season with Barcelona.

THE GIRLFRIEND

When Neymar was introduced as the new Barcelona star in June 2013, he was accompanied by his fiancée Bruna Marquezine. She was young, like Neymar—just barely 18 years of age. Despite her youth, Bruna is a well-known actress in Brazil and has played numerous roles in Brazilian soap operas from a young age. She couldn't fight her tears when she witnessed her boyfriend fulfill his dream as he put on his "blaugrana" (blue and deep red) Barcelona jersey.

THE FUTURE

The young boy from São Vicente has made it far in the world. His incredible skills and intelligence in the game have placed him among the very greatest. Whether Neymar will continue to grow and develop is now down to mental strength and endurance. He has speed and skill and he is incredibly eager to help his club and country win success. His understanding of the game is already at a high level, and will doubtlessly improve in the future.

If things continue as they are, Neymar can reach the heights men like Pelé, Maradona, and Cruyff have achieved, and where Messi is now. Neymar has everything it takes. He is now Messi's teammate and they have quickly begun a great partnership. It is truly a pleasure to observe them as they bring down the defenses of their opponents.

However, during the 2014 World Cup, Messi and Neymar became adversaries! They both wore the number 10 jersey! Though Neymar's dream of winning the world championship with Brazil did not come true, it is clear that Neymar will continue to bring joy to soccer fans with his brilliance in the coming years.

Neymar in the company of the best: Lionel Messi and the one and only Pelé. The picture was taken when Messi received the Ballon d'Or in January 2012; Neymar was also awarded.

Someday Neymar will raise this trophy!

"I am always trying
to improve everything—
dribbling, shooting,
headers, guiding the ball.
One can always improve!"

Learn more about Neymar!

Books
- Caioli, Luca, *Neymar: The Making of the World's Greatest New Number 10*
- Part, Michael, *Neymar the Wizard*

Websites
- Neymar has a comprehensive official website in Portuguese: neymaroficial.com/nav/
- FC Barcelona has a fine website in Spanish and English, with a special section on Neymar: fcbarcelona.com/all-about-neymar
- The Wikipedia entry on Neymar also holds an abundance of information about the player, his teams, and his career in general.
- This website is packed with information about Neymar and Brazil's national team: sambafoot.com/en/

Glossary

Striker: A forward player positioned closest to the opposing goal who has the primary role of receiving the ball from his teammates and delivering it to the goal.

Winger: Players who keep to the margins of the field and receive the ball from midfielders or defenders and send it forward to where the strikers await.

Offensive midfielder: They are positioned behind the team's forwards and see to taking the ball through the opposing defense, where they either pass to the strikers or attempt a goal themselves. This position is sometimes called "number 10" in reference to the Brazilian genius Pelé, who more or less created this position and wore shirt number 10.

Defensive midfielder: Plays more or less in front of his team's defense and whose central role is to break the offense of the opposing team and deliver the ball to the forwards of his own team. The contribution of these players is not always obvious, but they nevertheless play an important part in the game.

Central midfielder: The role of the central midfielder is divided between offense and defense, but mainly they seek to secure the center of the field for their team. Box-to-box midfielders are versatile players who possess such strength and oversight that they constantly spring between the penalty areas.

Fullbacks (either leftbacks or rightbacks): Players who defend the sides of the field, near their own goal, but they also dash up the field and overlap with wingers in order to lob the ball into the opponent's goal. The fullbacks are sometimes titled wingbacks if they are expected to play a bigger role in the offense.

Centerbacks: These players are the primary defenders of their teams, and are two or three in number depending on formation. The purpose of the centerback is first and foremost to prevent the opponents from scoring and then send the ball toward the center.

Sweeper: The purpose of the sweeper was to keep to the back of the defending teammates and "sweep up" the ball if they happened to lose it, but also to take the ball forward. The position of the sweeper has now been replaced by defensive midfielders.

Goalkeeper: Prevents the opponent's goals and is the only player who is allowed to use his hands!

CHOOSE THE TEAM

Coach:

_____

Who do you want on the field with Neymar? You pick the team and you can choose whoever you want and in whatever position. You can even choose yourself and your friends if you like! And don't forget the coach!

Goalkeeper:

_____

Right back:

_____

Left back:

_____

Defender:

_____

Defender:

_____

Midfielder:

_____

Midfielder:

_____

Midfielder:

_____

Forward:

_____

Forward:

Neymar

Forward: